AF481102

My Brother and Me

ISBN: 979-8211533332 (Paperback)
ISBN: 979-8-218-19415-4 (Hardcover)

Library of Congress Control Number: 2023907328

Art by Mariam Sherif Fadel

Printed in United States of America.

First printing edition 2023.

Dedicated to Aly and Adam

My name is Adam and I'm three.
My brother is Aly. He's older than me.

My dad lifts Adam high up into a tree.
I'm down below. There's no room for me.

Aly can write. Aly can read.
Why, oh why, can't I succeed?

Everyone thinks Adam is so cute.
Can't they see me in my suit?

River Race

I'm too short to go on the slide.
How is it fair that only Aly gets to ride?

I get in trouble, but Adam started the fight.
Why can't they see this isn't right?

You should know better.
Adam is little.
NO
NO
NO

Aly wins every game.
All I ever feel is shame.

I WIN
I win
I Win
I win
Iwin

I can't help but feel jealous.
When I tell my mom, she says,

"You're my first child.
I love you even when you're wild.

You can write, read, draw, and swim.
There's so much you teach him!

You're so polite.
You know what's right.

Allah made you an older brother.
He knows that Adam would not be better off
with any other.

For every good he learned from you
Your reward will accrue.

We love you and he loves you too.
We're so blessed to have you."

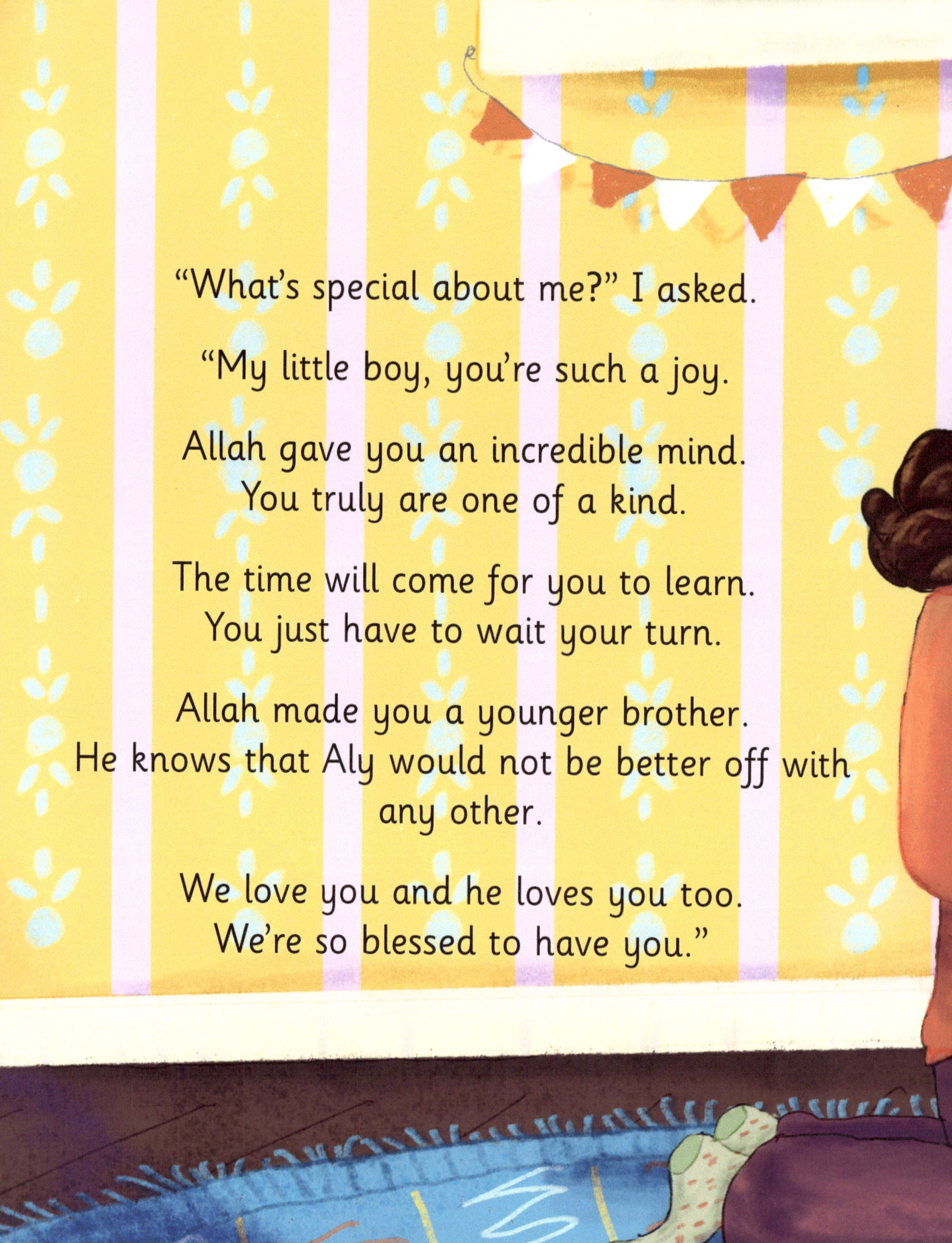

"What's special about me?" I asked.

"My little boy, you're such a joy.

Allah gave you an incredible mind.
You truly are one of a kind.

The time will come for you to learn.
You just have to wait your turn.

Allah made you a younger brother.
He knows that Aly would not be better off with
any other.

We love you and he loves you too.
We're so blessed to have you."

My dad lifts Adam high up into a tree.
I love it when it's us three.

Aly can write. Aly can read.
I'm happy to see him succeed.

Everyone thinks Adam is so cute.
It's true. Especially when he's in a suit.

River Race

I'm too short to go on the slide.
I'll watch Aly. At least he gets to ride.

I get in trouble, but Adam started the fight.
I'll set a good example and it'll be alright.

Don't cry
You can
take it

Aly wins every game.
He really does have great aim.

I win
I win
I win
I win
I win
I win

I love my brother and he loves me.
Thank you Allah for our family.
I promise to be the best version of me.
I'll be the brother You created me to be.

GLOSSARY

Allah: The Arabic word for God.